100

things you should know about

DEADLY CREATURES

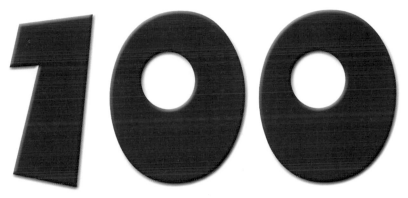

100

things you should know about

DEADLY CREATURES

Camilla de la Bedoyere

Consultant: Steve Parker

Miles Kelly
PUBLISHING

First published in 2007 by Miles Kelly Publishing Ltd
Bardfield Centre, Great Bardfield, Essex, CM7 4SL

2 4 6 8 10 9 7 5 3 1

Editorial Director: Belinda Gallagher
Art Director: Jo Brewer
Editor: Amanda Askew
Volume Designer: Candice Bekir
Indexer: Jane Parker
Reprographics: Anthony Cambray, Liberty Newton, Ian Paulyn
Production Manager: Elizabeth Brunwin

ISBN 978-1-84236-848-0

Printed in China

British Library Cataloguing-in-Publication Data
A catalogue record for this book is available from the British Library

ACKNOWLEDGEMENTS

The publishers would like to thank the following artists
who have contributed to this book:
Richard Draper, Mike Foster, Ian Jackson,
Steve Roberts, Eric Rowe, Mike Saunders
Cover artwork: Ian Jackson

All other artworks are from the Miles Kelly Artwork Bank

The publishers would like to thank the following
sources for the use of their photographs:
Page 11 Carlton Mceachern/Fotolia.com; 19 BRUCE DAVIDSON/naturepl.com;
21 Eric Gevaert/Fotolia.com; 31 NHPA/DANIEL HEUCLINGevaert/Fotolia.com;
29 Ami Beyer/Fotolia.com; 33 MARK MOFFETT/Minden Pictures/FLPA;
34 Reiner Weidemann/Fotolia.com; 38 FLPA; 45 NHPA/MARTIN HARVEY;
46 Photolibrary Group LTD

All other photographs are from:
Castrol, Corel, digitalSTOCK, digitalvision, John Foxx, PhotoAlto,
PhotoDisc, PhotoEssentials, PhotoPro, Stockbyte

www.mileskelly.net
info@mileskelly.net

Contents

A fight to survive

1 **The world is full of animals that are fighting to survive.** There are many reasons why animals may attack one another. Some are called predators and they kill for food. Others only kill to defend themselves, their young or their homes. Whatever the reason for using their claws, jaws, poisons or stings, these creatures are fascinating, but deadly.

▼ To catch its prey, the Nile crocodile lies very still in the water until the gazelle comes close. Then it shoots out of its hiding place, trying to catch the gazelle in its powerful jaws.

Killer carnivores

◀ False vampire bats have very sharp teeth, like the vampire bat. They catch and feed on frogs, mice, birds and other bats.

2 **Animals that eat meat are called carnivores.** Scavengers are carnivores that steal meat from others, or find dead animals to eat. Most carnivores, however, have to hunt and kill. These animals are called predators.

3 **Killer whales are some of the largest predators in the world.** Despite their size, these mighty beasts often hunt in groups called pods. By working together, killer whales can kill large animals, including other whales. However, they usually hunt smaller creatures, such as sea lions and dolphins.

▼ Anacondas are types of boa, and are the heaviest snakes in the world. As they don't have chewing teeth, snakes swallow their prey whole. Anacondas feed on large rodents called capybara, deer, fish and birds.

4 **Vampire bats do not eat meat, but they do feed on other animals.** With their razor-sharp teeth, vampire bats pierce the skin of a sleeping animal, such as a horse or pig, and drink their blood. False vampire bats are bigger, and they eat the flesh of other animals.

5 With their cold eyes and gaping mouths, piranhas are fierce-looking predators. When a shoal, or group, of piranhas attack, they work together like an enormous slicing machine. Within minutes, they can strip a horse to its skeleton using their tiny triangular teeth.

▲ Red piranhas are aggressive, speedy predators. They work together in a group to attack their prey, such as birds.

6 Some snakes rely on venom, or poison, to kill their prey, but constrictors squeeze their victims to death. Pythons and boas wrap their enormous bodies around the victim. Every time the captured animal breathes out, the snake squeezes a little tighter, until its prey can no longer breathe.

Lethal weapons

7 Many animals have deadly weapons, including teeth, claws, horns and stings. They are perfect for killing prey, or fighting enemies.

8 Inside the mouth of a meat-eating predator is an impressive collection of deadly daggers – teeth. Different teeth do different jobs. Canines, or fangs, are long and knife-like, and are used to grab prey or pierce skin. Teeth at the front of the mouth are very sharp, and are ideal for cutting and slicing flesh.

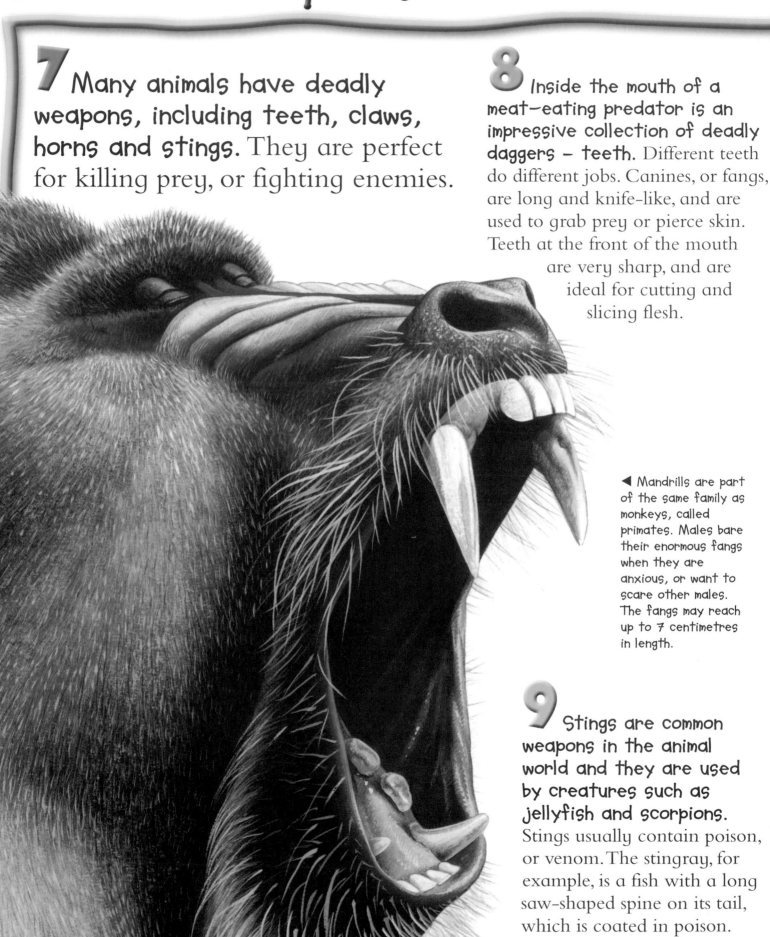

◄ Mandrills are part of the same family as monkeys, called primates. Males bare their enormous fangs when they are anxious, or want to scare other males. The fangs may reach up to 7 centimetres in length.

9 Stings are common weapons in the animal world and they are used by creatures such as jellyfish and scorpions. Stings usually contain poison, or venom. The stingray, for example, is a fish with a long saw-shaped spine on its tail, which is coated in poison.

10 Elephant and walrus tusks are overgrown teeth that make fearsome weapons when used to stab and lunge at attackers. Males use their tusks to fight one another at mating time, or to scare away predators. An elephant can kill a person with a single thrust from its mighty tusks.

FIND YOUR FANGS

You have cutting and chewing teeth, too. Use a mirror to find them.

Incisors are the sharp, flat teeth at the front of your mouth. They are used for cutting and tearing food.

Canines are the pointy teeth next to the incisors, used for piercing food.

Molars are at the back of your mouth. They are used for grinding food.

▼ Birds of prey grab hold of their victim with powerful talons, which pierce the flesh with ease.

▼ Cats have sharp claws that can be pulled back into the paws when they are not being used.

11 Eagles have huge claws called talons. The bird grasps prey in its feet, killing it by piercing and squeezing with its talons. Eagles and other carnivorous (meat-eating) birds are called birds of prey.

12 Some animals fight for mates, or territory (the area they live in). Horned animals, such as deer, are not predators, but they may fight and attack other animals. These animals have been known to harm humans when they are scared.

▲ Ibex are wild goats. They use their thick, curved horns to fight for mates or territory. Horns can be used to stab, wound and even kill.

Silent hunters

13 Agile and fast, with sharp teeth and claws, cats are some of the deadliest predators in the world. Most cats hunt alone, but lions works as a team to catch their prey.

14 A group of lions is called a pride, and the females are the hunters. Cubs spend hours play-fighting. This helps them to practise the skills they will need to catch and kill prey when they are older.

15 In Asia, many people are fearful of living near tigers. However, tigers hunt small creatures, such as birds, monkeys and reptiles. They have been known to attack bigger animals, such as rhinos and elephants, but it is rare for them to kill humans.

▼ Lionesses hunt in a group, which means they can attack big, aggressive animals, such as buffaloes.

16 Cheetahs are the fastest hunters on land, and can reach speeds of more than 100 kilometres an hour. Despite their great speed, cheetahs often fail to catch the animal they are chasing. Although these cats have great spurts of energy, they tire very quickly. If cheetahs have not caught their prey in about 30 seconds, it may escape – this time.

17 Leopards are secretive killers. They live throughout Africa and Asia, but are rarely seen. They are agile climbers and spend much of their time in trees, waiting for unsuspecting animals to wander by. Like most cats, leopards kill prey by sinking their huge teeth into the victim's neck.

Big, bold and beastly

18 Big, white and fluffy, polar bears look cuddly, but they are **deadly predators.** Occasionally, polar bears travel from the icy Arctic to small towns in search of food. At these times, they are hungry and dangerous, and may attack.

19 Polar bears use their **huge paws to swim with ease underwater.** They can hold their breath for several minutes, waiting until the time is right to swim up and grab their prey. On land, these ferocious bears hunt by creeping up on their prey, then pouncing, leaving the victim with no escape.

▼ A polar bear's paw is as big as a dinner plate, and is equipped with five big claws, one on each toe.

◄ Polar bears are meat eaters. They wait by a seal's breathing hole for the seal to appear above the water. With one swift bite, the bear kills its prey and drags it out of the water.

QUIZ

1. Which bear would you find in the Arctic?

2. Which fairytale character ate the three bears' porridge?

3. Which slippery creatures do brown bears like to eat?

Answers:
1. Polar bear 2. Goldilocks
3. Salmon

▲ Kodiak bears live in Alaska where they eat fish, grass, plants and berries. They only bare their teeth and roar to defend themselves against predators.

20 Brown bears are one of the largest meat eaters in the world, and can stand more than 3 metres tall. They are powerful animals, with long front claws and strong jaws.

▶ Brown bears catch salmon as they leap out of the water. A snap of the jaws is enough to grab the wriggling fish.

21 Grizzlies are brown bears of North America. They often come into contact with humans when searching for food and raiding rubbish bins, and are considered to be extremely dangerous. Grizzlies often live in woods and forests. They mainly feed on berries, fruit, bulbs and roots, but also fish for salmon in fast-flowing rivers.

22 Black bears in Asia rarely attack humans, but when they do, the attack is often fatal. Asian black bears are herbivores. This means that they eat plants rather than meat. If they are scared, these shy animals may attack to kill.

Skills to kill

23 Monkeys and apes belong to the same group of animals as humans, called **primates**. These intelligent creatures have great skills of communication and teamwork. Although monkeys, gorillas and chimps appear to be playful, they can be dangerous.

24 It was once believed that chimps only ate plants and insects. However, it has been discovered that groups of chimps ambush and attack colobus monkeys. Each chimp takes its own role in the hunting team. During the chase, the chimps communicate with each other by screeching and hooting.

25 Chimps also kill each other. Groups of male chimps patrol the forest, looking for males from another area. If they find one, the group may gang up on the stranger and kill him.

▶ Chimps use their great intelligence to organize hunts. Some of them scream, hoot and chase the colobus monkey. Other chimps in the group hide, ready to attack.

26 Baboons live in family groups and eat a wide range of foods, from seeds to antelopes. Young males eventually leave their family, and fight with other males to join a new group and find mates.

27 A mighty gorilla may seem fierce, but it is actually one of the most gentle primates. Large adult males, called silverbacks, only charge to protect their families by scaring other animals, or humans, away. Gorillas can inflict terrible bite wounds with their fearsome fangs.

I DON'T BELIEVE IT!

Chimps are skilled at making and using tools. It is easy for them to hold sticks and rocks in their hands. They use sticks to break open insects' nests and they use rocks to smash nuts.

Canine killers

28 Wolves, coyotes and African hunting dogs belong to the dog family. Most live and hunt in groups, or packs. By working together, a pack can attack and kill large prey, such as deer and bison.

◄ When a wolf feels threatened, the fur on its back, called its hackles, stands on end. This makes it look bigger and fiercer.

29 Wolves have excellent senses of sight, hearing and smell to help them to find their prey. These strong, agile creatures have been known to travel a distance of 100 kilometres in just one night in search of food.

30 Coyotes are wild dogs that live in North America. They normally hunt in pairs or on their own, although they may join together as a group to chase large prey, such as deer.

31 Like wild cats, coyotes hunt by keeping still and watching an animal nearby. They wait for the right moment, then creep towards their prey and pounce, landing on top of the startled victim. Coyotes are swift runners and often chase jackrabbits across rocks and up hills.

BE A WOLF!

1. One person is Mr Wolf and stands with their back to the other players.
2. The players stand 10 paces away and shout, "What's the time, Mr Wolf?".
3. If Mr Wolf shouts, "It's 10 o'clock", the players take 10 steps towards Mr Wolf.
4. Watch out because when Mr Wolf shouts "Dinnertime", he chases the other players and whoever he catches is out of the game!

▶ When African hunting dogs pursue their prey, such as the wildebeest, the chase may go on for several kilometres, but the dogs rarely give up. They wait until their prey tires, then leap in for the kill.

32 African wild dogs are deadly pack hunters. They work as a team to chase and torment their prey. The whole pack shares the meal, tearing at the meat with their sharp teeth.

Ambush and attack

33 **Lurking beneath the surface of the water, a deadly hunter waits, ready to pounce.** Lying absolutely still, only its eyes and nostrils are visible. With one swift movement, the victim is dragged underwater. This killer is the crocodile, a relative of the dinosaurs.

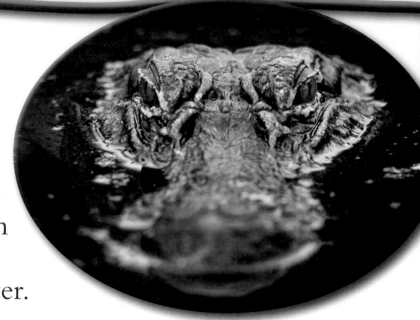

▲ Crocodiles and alligators are well-suited to their aquatic lifestyle. They spend much of their day in water, keeping cool and hidden from view.

Only teeth in the upper jaw are visible

Alligator

▲▼ When a crocodile's mouth is closed, some of the teeth on its lower jaw can be seen. Alligators have wide u-shaped jaws, but the jaws of crocodiles are narrow and v-shaped.

Teeth in the lower jaw can be seen

Crocodile

34 **When a crocodile has its prey in sight, it moves at lightning speed.** The prey has little chance to escape as the crocodile pulls it underwater. Gripping the victim in its mighty jaws, the crocodile twists and turns in a 'deathspin' until its victim has drowned.

35 **The largest crocodiles in the world live in estuaries, where rivers meet the oceans.** They are called estuarine crocodiles and can reach a staggering 7 metres in length. These giant predators are often known as man-eating crocodiles, although they are most likely to catch turtles, snakes, monkeys, cows and pigs.

36 Alligators are very strong reptiles with wide jaws and thick, scaly skin on their backs. They live in marshes, ponds and rivers, often close to where people live. Like all crocodiles and alligators, the American alligator will catch and eat anything. They have even been known to attack humans.

▼ Crocodiles and alligators have huge jaws, full of teeth. As well as being used for grabbing and holding prey, they use their teeth to slice pieces from the body of the victim.

I DON'T BELIEVE IT!

Crocodiles and alligators store their uneaten food underwater for several weeks. The remains rot, making it easier for the reptiles to swallow. Yum!

Ravenous raptors

37 Eagles, hawks, kites and ospreys are fearsome predators called birds of prey. Equipped with incredible eyesight, powerful legs, and sharp claws and bills, they hunt during the day, soaring high in the sky as they look for food.

38 Birds of prey are also known as raptors, which comes from the Latin word 'rapere', meaning 'to seize'. Once they have captured their prey, such as a mouse, bird or frog, a raptor usually takes it to its nest to start pulling off fur and feathers. Bones are also thrown away, and the ground near a raptor's nest may be strewn with animal remains.

▶ Like most birds of prey, golden eagles have razor-sharp, hooked bills. They use them to tear the body of their prey apart.

▶ Eagle owls are large, powerful birds. They hunt and capture large animals, including other owls and birds of prey.

39 Birds do not have teeth. They have bills, or beaks, instead. Tearing large pieces of meat is a difficult job using just a bill. Birds of prey use their curved claws, called talons, to hold or rip their food apart, or they just swallow it whole.

40 Little more than the flap of a wing can be heard as an owl swoops down to grab an unsuspecting mouse. Owls hunt at night. They can even see small movements on the ground, thanks to their large eyes and sharp eyesight. When they hunt in total darkness, they rely on their excellent sense of hearing to find food.

41 Peregrine falcons are the fastest hunters in the world, reaching speeds of up to 230 kilometres an hour as they swoop down to attack other birds. Peregrines hunt on the wing. This means that they catch their prey while in flight. They chase their prey to tire it out, before lashing out with their sharp talons.

▼ Bald eagles live on a diet of fish, which they swipe out of the water using their talons.

42 Ospreys dive, feet–first, into the water from a great height in pursuit of their prey. Fish may be slippery, but ospreys have spiky scales on the underside of the feet so they can grip more easily. Once ospreys have a fish firmly in their grasp, they fly away to find a safe place to eat.

Mighty monsters

43 **Not all deadly creatures kill for food.** Many of them only attack when they are frightened. Some plant-eating animals fight to protect their young, or when they feel scared.

44 Hippos may appear calm when they are wallowing at the edge of a waterhole, but they kill more people in Africa than any other large animal. These huge creatures fiercely protect their own stretch of water, and females are extremely aggressive when they have calves and feel threatened.

45 **African buffaloes can be very aggressive towards other animals and humans.** If they become scared, they move quickly and attack with their huge horns. Groups of buffaloes surround a calf or ill member of the herd to protect it. They face outwards to prevent predators getting too close.

46 If an elephant starts flapping its ears and trumpeting, it is giving a warning sign to stay away. However, when an elephant folds its ears back, curls its trunk under its mouth and begins to run — then it really means business. Elephants will attack to keep other animals or humans away from the infants in their herd, and males will fight one another for a mate.

47 With huge bodies and massive horns, rhinos look like fearsome predators. They are actually related to horses and eat a diet of leaves, grass and fruit. Rhinos can become aggressive, however, when they are scared. They have poor eyesight, which may be why they can easily feel confused or threatened, and attack without warning.

◄ Male hippos fight one another using their massive teeth as weapons. Severe injuries can occur, leading to the death of at least one of the hippos.

I DON'T BELIEVE IT!

Adult male elephants are called bulls, and they can become killers. A single stab from an elephant's tusk is enough to cause a fatal wound, and one elephant is strong enough to flip a car over onto its side!

Toxic tools

▶ Marine toads are the largest toads in the world. When they are threatened, venom oozes from the glands in the toad's skin. This poison could kill a small animal in minutes.

48 Some animals rely on teeth and claws to kill prey, but others have an even deadlier weapon called venom. Venom is the name given to any poison that is made by an animal's body. There are lots of different types of venom. Some cause only a painful sting, but others can result in death.

▼ The death stalker scorpion is one of the most dangerous scorpions in the world. It lives in North Africa and the Middle East. One sting can cause paralysis (loss of movement) and heart failure in humans.

49 The marine toad produces venom from special areas, called glands, behind its eyes. The venom is not used to kill prey, but to protect the toad from being eaten by other animals because it is extremely poisonous if swallowed.

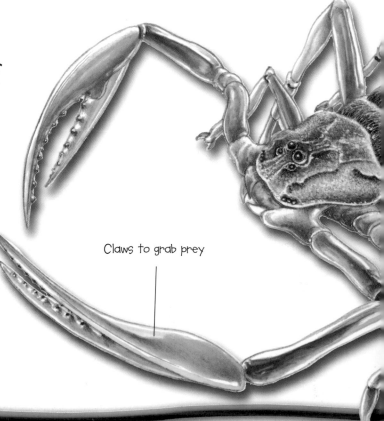

Claws to grab prey

50
Many snakes have venom glands in their mouths. They use their fangs to inject poison straight into their victim's body. Venom is made from saliva mixed with deadly substances. Spitting cobras shoot venom from their mouths. This venom can cause blindness in humans.

51
Scorpions belong to the same group as spiders – arachnids. Instead of producing venom in their fangs, they have stings in their tails. They use venom to kill prey, such as lizards and mice, or to defend themselves. Few scorpions can cause serious injury to humans, but some, such as the death stalker scorpion, are deadly.

52
Even small insects can harm other animals. Hornets, wasps and bees have stings in their tails that are attached to venom sacs. A single sting causes swelling and pain, and may prove fatal to people who are allergic to the venom.

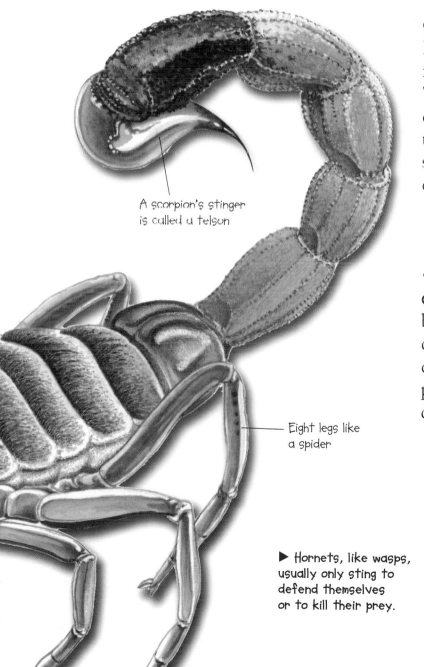

A scorpion's stinger is called a telson

Eight legs like a spider

▶ Hornets, like wasps, usually only sting to defend themselves or to kill their prey.

Sting

Scary snakes

► Venomous snakes, such as the rattlesnake, inject venom using their large fangs. Snakes use their venom to paralyze (stop all movement) or kill their prey.

Venom runs down the groove on the outside of the fangs and is then injected into the victim's body

54 Cobras kill more than 10,000 people in India every year. As a warning sign, cobras spread their neck ribs, or hoods, to make them look more fearsome. Then they quickly lunge forwards and sink their fangs into their prey.

53 With unblinking eyes, sharp fangs and flickering tongues, snakes look like menacing killers. Despite their fearsome reputation, snakes only attack people when they feel threatened.

55 The taipan is one of Australia's most venomous snakes. When this snake attacks, it injects large amounts of venom that can kill a person in less than an hour.

56 Carpet vipers are small snakes found throughout many parts of Africa and Asia. They are responsible for hundreds, maybe thousands, of human deaths every year. Carpet viper venom affects the nervous system and the blood, causing the victim to bleed to death.

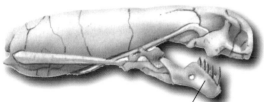

◀ Primitive snakes have a heavy skull with a short lower jaw and few teeth.

Short jaw that cannot open very wide

◀ Rear-fanged snakes have fangs in the roof of their mouths.

Fangs are towards the rear of the mouth, below the eye

57 Gaboon vipers have the longest fangs of any snake, reaching 5 centimetres in length. They produce large amounts of venom, which they inject deeply into the flesh with dagger-like teeth. Although slow and calm by nature, Gaboon vipers attack with great speed and a single bite can kill a human in less than two hours.

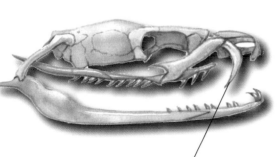

◀ Some snakes have fangs at the front of their mouths.

The fangs are hollow, and positioned at the front of the mouth

▶ Snakes kill their prey with a lethal bite. Then they swallow the victim, such as a rodent, whole.

Dragons and monsters

▼ Komodo dragons use their powerful jaws to tear the flesh of their victim, and then eat everything, including bones and fur.

58 **Komodo dragons are not really dragons, but lizards.** They can reach 3 metres in length and up to 100 kilograms in weight, making them the largest lizards in the world. They hunt their prey using their sensitive sense of smell.

59 **Once the Komodo has caught its prey, it sinks its sharp teeth into the victim's flesh.** With a mouth full of poisonous bacteria, one bite is enough to kill an animal with an infection, even if it escapes the Komodo's clutches.

QUIZ

1. What colour is the Gila monster?
2. Why does the fire salamander have bold patterns on its skin?
3. How does the Komodo dragon hunt its prey?

Answers:
1. Black, pink and yellow 2. To warn predators that it is poisonous 3. Using its sensitive sense of smell

60 There are only two truly poisonous lizards – the Gila monster and the Mexican beaded lizard. Gila monsters live in North America and they have bands of black, pink and yellow on their scaly skin to warn predators to stay away.

▲ Gila monsters use their sense of smell to hunt small animals and find reptile eggs. They can kill their prey with a single bite.

▼ Fire salamanders are amphibians, like frogs. They hunt insects and earthworms, mainly at night.

61 Fire salamanders look like a cross between a lizard and a frog. They have bold patterns on their skin to warn predators that they are poisonous. The poison, or toxin, is on their skin and tastes foul. They squirt the toxin at predators, irritating or even killing them.

Fearsome frogs

62 **At first glance, few frogs appear fearsome.** They may not have teeth or claws, but frogs and toads produce a deadly substance in their moist skin. This substance may taste foul or even be poisonous. The most poisonous frogs live in the forests of Central and South America. They are called poison-dart frogs.

63 **One of the deadliest frogs is the golden poison-dart frog.** It lives in rainforests in western Colombia, and its skin produces a very powerful poison – one of the deadliest known substances. A single touch is enough to cause almost instant death.

▶ The male green poison-dart frog carries tadpoles on his back. He takes them to a safe place in water where they will grow into adults.

▼ The strawberry poison-dart frog is also known as the 'blue jeans' frog because of its blue legs.

64 **Many poison-dart frogs are becoming rare in the wild.** This is because the rainforests where they live are being cut down. Some poison-dart frogs can be kept in captivity, where they gradually become less poisonous. When they are raised in captivity, these frogs are not poisonous at all.

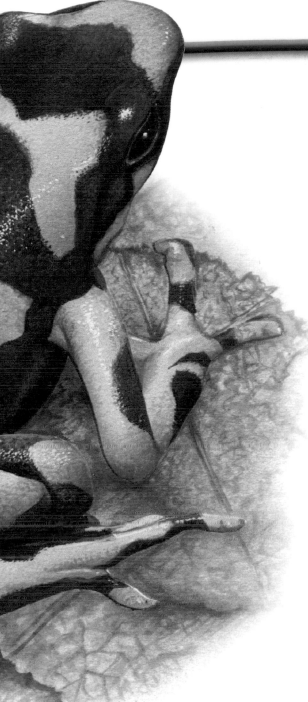

65 People who live in the rainforests of Central and South America use the poison from frogs to catch food. A hunter wipes the tip of a dart on the poisonous frog's back, then carefully puts it in a blowpipe. One puff sends the lethal dart into the body of an unsuspecting monkey or bird.

▼ Poison is wiped off the back of the golden poison-dart frog with a dart. One frog produces enough poison for more than 50 darts.

66 Looking after eggs is the job of male green poison-dart frogs. The female lays her eggs amongst the leaf litter on the forest floor. The male guards them until they hatch into tadpoles, then carries them to water, where they will grow into frogs.

Eight-legged hunters

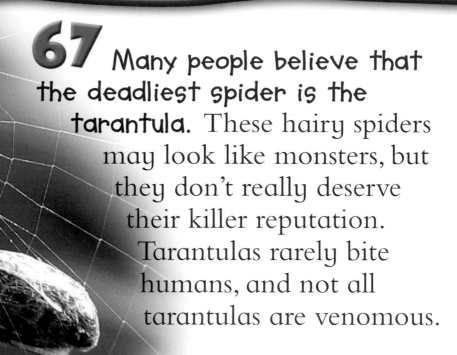

67 Many people believe that the deadliest spider is the tarantula. These hairy spiders may look like monsters, but they don't really deserve their killer reputation. Tarantulas rarely bite humans, and not all tarantulas are venomous.

▲ After an insect becomes trapped in the spider's web, the spider kills it with a venomous bite. The spider will eat almost every part of its prey.

69 Tarantulas hunt their prey, such as insects, frogs and lizards, rather than spinning webs. They use their large fangs to inject venom into their prey and crush it into a pulp. Digestive juices are poured over the victim until it turns into a liquid and can be sucked up.

68 Black widow spiders are one of the most dangerous spiders in the world, but they only attack if disturbed. A bite from a male is nothing to worry about, but a bite from a female may prove fatal.

◀ Female black widow spiders use their poison not only to catch prey, but also to kill their partners after mating.

70 Spiders belong to a group of animals called arachnids, along with scorpions and ticks. Some ticks can kill without using deadly poison. They attach themselves to the bodies of humans and other animals, and suck their blood. This can spread deadly diseases.

QUIZ

1. How do ticks kill animals?
2. Is the male or female black widow spider more dangerous?
3. Which spider stands on its hind legs when it feels threatened?

Answers:
1. They suck their blood and spread diseases 2. Female 3. Funnel web spider

71 There are many types of funnel web spider, and some of them are very venomous. When a funnel web spider is threatened, it stands on its hind legs and rears, showing its huge fangs. These killers bite their prey many times, injecting poison.

▲ The fangs of the funnel web spider are so strong that they can pierce human skin, even fingernails. Its bite can cause death in just 15 minutes.

Clever defenders

72 To survive in a dangerous world, animals need to be able to hide, fight, or appear deadly. When it is threatened, the spiny puffer fish swallows large amounts of water, making its body swell up and its spines stand on end.

73 Spines can be used to pass venom into the victim's body, or used as weapons of defence. The long, sharp spines on the Cape porcupine are called quills, and they stick into an attacker's body, causing painful injuries.

▼▶ The spiny puffer fish stiffens and swells its body, changing from an ordinary-looking fish to a spiky ball.

◄ Tortoises are protected from predators by their tough shell. Even the sharp claws and teeth of lion cubs cannot break it.

74
Some animals hide from their predators using camouflage. This means the colour or pattern of an animal's skin blends in with its surroundings. Lizards called chameleons are masters of camouflage. They can change their skin colour from brown to green so they blend in with their background. They do this to communicate with one another.

75
The bold colours and pattern on the coral snake's skin warns predators that it is poisonous. The milk snake looks almost identical to the coral snake, but it is not venomous. Its colour keeps it safe though, because predators think it is poisonous.

I DON'T BELIEVE IT!

Electric eels have an unusual way of staying safe – they zap prey and predators with electricity! They can produce 600 volts of power at a time, which is enough to kill a human!

► The harmless milk snake looks similar to the venomous coral snake, so predators stay away. This life–saving animal trick is called mimicry.

76 Deep in the ocean lurk some of the deadliest creatures in the world. There are keen-eyed killers, venomous stingers and sharp-toothed hunters, but as few of these animals come into contact with humans, attacks are rare.

▶ The Australian box jellyfish is also known as the sea wasp. Its tentacles can grow more than 3 metres in length and one animal has enough venom to kill 60 people.

77 Barracudas are long, strong, powerful fish. They lunge at their prey, baring dagger-like teeth. Although they prey on other fish, barracudas may mistake swimmers for food and attack them.

78 The box jellyfish is one of the most lethal creatures in the world. A touch from only one tentacle can kill a human. The floating body of a jellyfish is harmless, but danger lies in the many tentacles that drift below. Each tentacle is covered with tiny stingers that shoot venom into the victim.

◀ Barracudas are fierce fish with powerful jaws and sharp teeth.

79 A Portuguese man o'war may look like a single animal, but actually it is made up of many creatures, called polyps. A gas-filled chamber floats on the water's surface and long tendrils, each measuring 20 metres or more, hang below. The tendrils have venomous stings that catch food for the whole colony of polyps.

▲ Stingrays have stings in their tails that look like darts. They use them in defence to stab any animal that frightens them.

80 The most dangerous octopus in the world only measures 10 to 20 centimetres in length. The blue-ringed octopus grabs prey with its tentacles and then bites deeply injecting venom into the victim. The venom can kill a human in just four minutes.

▶ Shown here at actual size, the tiny blue-ringed octopus has enough venom to kill ten people.

81 Few animals send a shiver down the spine quite like a great white shark. This huge fish is a skilled hunter. Its bullet-shaped body can slice through the water at lightning speed, powered by huge muscles and a crescent-shaped tail.

82 Sharks are fish, and belong to the same family as rays and skates. Most sharks are predators and feed on fish, squid, seals and other sea creatures. Some sharks hunt with quick spurts of energy as they chase their prey. Others lie in wait for victims to pass by.

83 One of the deadliest sharks can be found in oceans and seas throughout the world. Blue sharks often hunt in packs and circle their prey before attacking. Although these creatures normally eat fish and squid, they will attack humans.

84 Bull sharks are a deadly threat to humans. This is because they live in areas close to human homes. They often swim inland, using the same rivers that people use to bathe and collect water, and may attack.

▲ Great white sharks are fearsome predators. They have rows of ultra-sharp triangular teeth that are perfect for taking large bites out of prey, such as seals, sea lions and dolphins.

85 Grey reef sharks are sleek, swift predators of the Indian and Pacific oceans. Unusually, they give plenty of warning before they attack. If the grey reef shark feels threatened, it drops its fins down, raises its snout and starts weaving and rolling through the water.

Peril at the shore

▼ When the stonefish's spines are touched, venom is released from the gland at the base. The venom can cause breathing difficulties and heart failure.

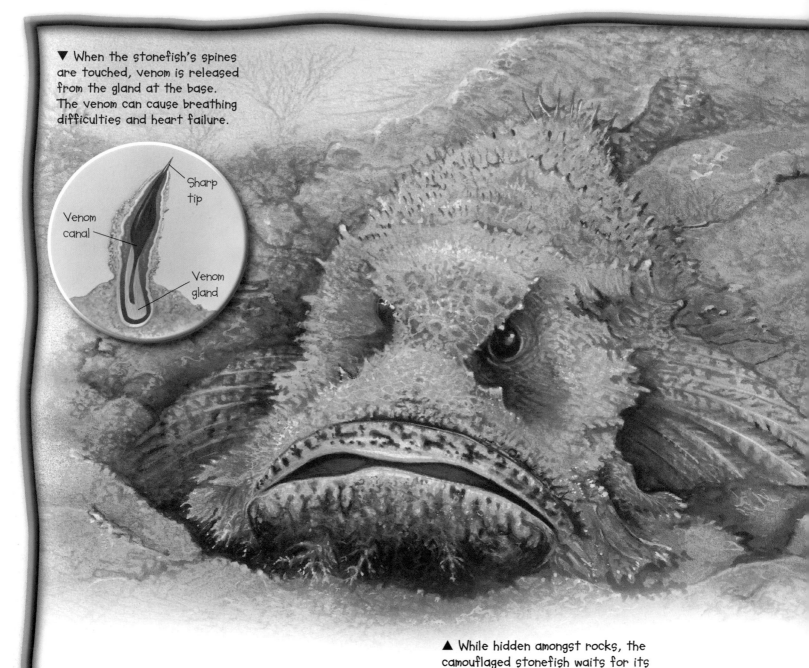

Sharp tip

Venom canal

Venom gland

▲ While hidden amongst rocks, the camouflaged stonefish waits for its prey, such as small fish.

86 The seashore may seem like a quiet place, but danger lies beneath the gently lapping waves. While some predators actively hunt their prey, some creatures just sit and wait.

87 Stonefish may look like a piece of rocky coral, but their cunning disguise hides a deadly surprise. One touch of the sharp spines on the stonefish's back results in an injection of venom, which may be fatal.

88 **Lionfish are graceful swimmers, but the long spines on their fins inject venom as swiftly as a needle.** A single injury from one spine causes immediate sickness and great pain, but it is unlikely to prove deadly to a human.

▼ Cone shells use their long proboscis to shoot a poisonous dart into their prey. The venom is very powerful and quickly paralyzes the prey.

89 **Sea snakes spend their lives in water.** They breathe air, so they need to keep returning to the surface. All sea snakes are poisonous, and although their bites are painless at first, the venom is very powerful and can kill.

90 **Seashells are not always as harmless as they appear.** Rather than chasing their prey, cone shells attack other animals using a poison that paralyzes the victim so it cannot escape. The venom of fish-eating cone shells can paralyze a fish within seconds. Although their venom can be fatal to humans, it is being used by scientists to develop medicines that reduce pain.

Minibeasts

◄ Although houseflies do not have stings, they are dangerous to humans. They can spread diseases if they land on food.

91 **Animals don't have to be big to be beastly.** There are many small animals, particularly insects, that are killers. Some of them, such as ants, are predators that hunt to eat. Others, such as locusts, cause destruction that affects humans.

92 Ants are found almost everywhere, **except in water.** Most ants are harmless to humans, but army ants and driver ants turn tropical forests and woodlands into battlefields. The stings of army ants contain chemicals that dissolve flesh. Once their prey has turned to liquid, the ants can begin to drink it.

▼ Millions of army ants live in a single group, or colony. They hunt together, swarming through leaf litter and attacking anything in their way.

93 Driver ants have large jaws that can slice easily through food. They hunt in large numbers and swarm through forests hunting for prey. Driver ants can kill large animals, such as cows, by biting them to death. They have also been known to strip a chicken down to its skeleton in less than a day.

94 Deadly plagues of locusts have been written about for thousands of years. When they search for food, they travel in swarms of millions, eating all the plants they encounter. This can leave humans without any food.

▲ Killer bees fiercely protect their hive by swarming around it. They will attack anything that approaches the nest.

95 Killer bees are a new type of bee that was created by a scientist. He was hoping to breed bees that made lots of honey, but the bees proved to be extremely aggressive. Killer bees swarm in huge groups and when one bee stings, the others quickly join in. One sting is not deadly, but lots of bee stings can kill a human. It is thought that about 1000 people have been killed by these minibeasts.

The enemy within

96 Many deadly creatures are too small to be seen. They are parasites, living on or inside the body of humans or animals, causing harm, disease and even death. An animal that is home to a parasite is called a host.

▼ The Black Death, or bubonic plague, was spread by rats and it wiped out one-third of Europe's population (25 million people) about 700 years ago.

97 Rats are known to spread disease. They carry bacteria on their paws and in their mouths, but they also carry another type of parasite called fleas. Even the fleas can have parasites inside their bodies – plague bacteria.

98 Humans have suffered from plagues for thousands of years. These diseases are spread when rat fleas bite people, spreading the plague bacteria. Plague usually only occurs when people live in dirty conditions where rats and their fleas can breed. Plague can spread quickly, wiping out millions of lives.

▼ Tsetse flies feed on blood and spread parasites that cause sleeping sickness. This painful disease is common in developing countries and leads to death if not treated.

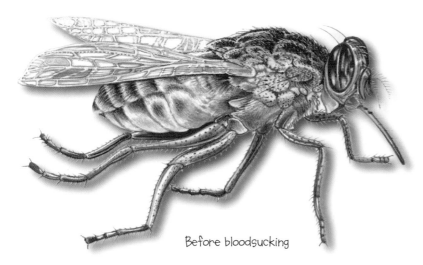

Before bloodsucking

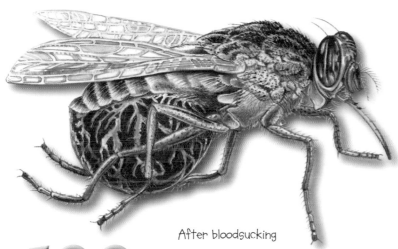

After bloodsucking

QUIZ

1. Which plague wiped out about one-third of Europe's population?
2. How do mosquitoes spread malaria and other diseases?
3. Which parasites do rats carry?

Answers:
1. The Black Death 2. By sucking the blood of their victims 3. Fleas

99 The mosquito and its tiny parasites are among the deadliest creatures in the world. When mosquitoes suck human and animal blood, they pass parasites into the host's body, including the parasite that causes malaria. Malaria is a disease that mainly affects people living in hot countries in the developing world. It causes about one million deaths a year in Africa.

100 Some of the most common parasites are worms. Tiny threadlike worms called nematodes live inside the bodies of most animals, including some humans. Nematodes can spread disease. Tapeworms belong to a different family of worms called flatworms. They absorb food from their host's intestine.

▶ Mosquitoes pierce the skin of the victim to suck their blood, spreading deadly diseases, such as malaria.

Index